27

Travis I. Sivart

27 Thoughts on Having No Regrets in Life

Travis I. Sivart

Travis I. Sivart

All rights reserved. This book or any portion thereof
may not be reproduced or used in any manner whatsoever
without the express written permission of the publisher
except for the use of brief quotations in a book review.

27 Thoughts for a Good Life
27 Thoughts on Life Series, Book 2

Copyright © 2017 Travis I. Sivart

Cover Design by Travis I. Sivart

All rights reserved.

ISBN 10: 1544106807
ISBN 13:9781544106809

Talk of the Tavern Publishing Group

Travis I. Sivart

Enjoying what you're reading?
Want a free eBook?

Go to
http://www.TravisISivart.com/FreeBook

Travis I. Sivart

27 Thoughts on Having No Regrets in Life

DEDICATION

This book is for my son, friends, and anyone else who listened to me spout ideas and suggestions I have learned.

27 Thoughts on Having No Regrets in Life

Table of Contents

Introduction xiii

1. Save Money 1
2. Pursue Your Dreams & Passions 3
3. Live Your Bucket List 5
4. Make Time for Friends & Family................................... 7
5. Live True to Yourself, Not Others 9
6. Work to Live, Don't Live to Work 11
7. Be Honest & Express Your Feelings 13
8. Confidence 15
9. Forgive & Forget More 17
10. Stand Up for Yourself... 19
11. Face Your Fears... 21
12. Don't Pursue What Runs Away............................... 23
13. Live in the Moment 25
14. Be Aware of Your Surroundings............................. 27
15. Learn to Listen 29
16. Know What You Want 31
17. Stay Clean, Dress Neatly 33

18. Learn to Speak 35

19. Be Prepared 37

20. Know Three Clean Jokes 39

21. Understand Your Goals, Large & Small 41

22. Clean as You Go 43

23. Avoid Extremes & Excess 45

24. Succeed & Fail with Grace 47

25. Use Manners & Common Courtesy 49

26. Breathe, Hydrate, & Sleep 51

27. Time Management 53

About the Author 57

Introduction

This is a book of advice, ugh. Ever notice the word vice is in advice, just preceded by the suffix of ad? Think about that, and then join me in the next paragraph.

Hey there, glad you made it this far. So, you see my ego in this? Advice is like fish, and opinions are like buttholes; Google that stuff and you'll see. Anyhow, this is stuff I have passed on to my own children, as well as friends – younger and older – when they are seeking counsel. Now, I pass it on in the form of a book.

Once upon a time, we would sit and listen to our elders, peers - or even the wisdom of children – and soak in timeless insight and experience. Of course, we would promptly ignore it, go out, and make the same mistakes they warned us about, and then sagely nod our heads about the advice, and pass it onto the next person willing to listen.

Well, this is a whole book of those pearls of wisdom. In no way is it a complete life guide, but it is the essentials as I see them. And to be clear, just because I know the value of these things, doesn't mean I am wise enough to follow them all. Good luck in being smarter than I am!

Travis I. Sivart

1. Save Money

Most folks know they have to work for a living, but what many never come to realize is that you have to save money if you ever want to stop needing to work so you can live, this includes retirement.

Our modern society has come to rely on loans for so many things; we have become accustomed to not owning our homes, cars, and even our basic electronics and appliances. I recommend you stop that trend, and the best way is learn to save.

I could write a whole book on this topic alone, and many others already have. The simple math is put away a minimum of 10% of any money you make, but 20% is much better. Don't touch it. This isn't for repairing your car, vacations, or anything else. This is money so you can stop working one day.

Use coupons, shop sales, buy generic in things you can, and don't buy tons of useless stuff you don't need. People with money follow these rules, and because of it they keep more of their money.

Oh, and whenever you can, pay cash. Especially for big purchases like your car or house. At least put down big down payments. The less you pay any finance charge, the more money you save.

Travis I. Sivart

2. Pursue Your Dreams & Passions

Life is meant to be enjoyed but balanced with our responsibilities. Too many people forget that. They go to work, come home, watch TV, eat dinner, and go to bed. On their days off they spend a little money and say that this must be happiness.

When we're younger we have passion and dreams. We play instruments, dance like crazy monkeys, write poetry, want to visit every corner of the world, act in movies, parachute, dive with dolphins, and so many other things. As many people get older they forget that they can still do these things. They find excuses like; not enough time, job is too demanding, kids make it impossible, can't afford it, and tons of other reasons.

The good news is that it doesn't have to be that way; you can still find time for what you love. The bad news is that you may have to give up other things to free up money and time to be able to live your dreams. You can't spend six hours in front of the TV or computer every night if you want to learn to play an instrument or learn a new language. You can't buy that overpriced car and still afford to travel to foreign countries.

The best news is that the choice of how you spend your time and money is up to you.

Travis I. Sivart

3. Live Your Bucket List

A little while back someone asked me what I would put on my bucket list. It took me over a week to come up with something, because everything I thought of I had already done. Even the couple of things I thought of that I hadn't done yet, I had in the planning stages. I was living my bucket list.

This relates to the previous entry, pursuing your dreams and passions, and they go hand in hand. So many folks wait until there is – what they perceive as – almost no time left in their lives to do the cool things that they've always talked about doing.

Make your bucket list - whether you're sixteen, sixty-six, or any other age – and begin checking things off by making them happen now. If you make a new list every ten years, you'll see it change as you change.

Don't wait until you feel like you're running out of time. Begin living life to the fullest. Today plan to do something you want to do tomorrow.

Travis I. Sivart

4. Make Time for Friends & Family

I don't know about you, but I have been estranged from my family. I watch others with their family and it makes me happy to see the community that has decades of roots that a family gives someone. As I got older and had a son of my own, I wanted him to have that also. When I realized I couldn't do it with blood relations, I turned to my friends.

A very old adage says, 'Friends are the family which you choose', and that is the truth if you choose your friends carefully. I have had friends that have done more for me than my family ever will, and I have done the same for others.

The point is, work is fine, but it is the people in your life that make it feel full, fun, and beautiful. Objects never give the pleasure that good company that cares about you and your well-being can give. Make time to spend with your family- whether that is your parents, cousins, spouse, children, siblings, or whoever – or your friends. These are the people who make any achievement feel even better. Take care of them first and foremost.

Travis I. Sivart

5. Live True to Yourself, Not Others

This one can be hard to understand until you have gone through a certain amount of challenges in life; on the other hand some folks are born understanding this. The old saying of "You can't make everyone happy" is key to this. The truth is; you can't make anyone happy except yourself.

Think that's wrong? Think about when you're in a bad mood and someone tries to cheer you up. If you don't want to be cheered up, they can't make you happy. Only when you choose to let them lift your spirits do things brighten up for you. You choose to let them make you happy, thus you made yourself happy by appreciating their efforts. Without your own consent to be happy, you would've stayed miserable and cranky.

Living true to yourself means taking care of yourself, living your dreams, and allowing yourself to be happy. Don't try to find happiness in making other people's lives better. If you're living true to yourself, then the people in your life will reap those benefits as a fringe benefit. But trying to live your life to make others happy is a plan doomed to failure in the long run.

Travis I. Sivart

6. Work to Live, Don't Live to Work

I covered a little bit of this in the friends and family part, but now I will cover this specific point more in depth. Work is part of life and gives us many things; money to spend on necessities and frivolities, a sense of identity, a feeling of accomplishment, a sense of community and belonging, and more. But rarely is it ultimately fulfilling.

As important as work is, it is merely a tool so you may enjoy life overall. If it consumes all your time and energy, you won't have either of those things when you are with people you love and doing the things you enjoy.

Always make time to enjoy the fruits of your labor. Otherwise, what was the point of the labor?

Travis I. Sivart

7. Be Honest & Express Your Feelings

When dealing with life it is often easier to be happy if you simply let the people around you know what you want and how you feel about something. Hiding your feelings only leads to an explosion, of some sort, later.

It is easy to lose opportunities just because you were too shy or nervous to step up and let people know that you want it, or don't want it.

This can be a fine line, and only practice and common sense can truly guide you in this. Being honest and expressing yourself is a selective thing, and knowing when to do it is as important as doing it. Don't bludgeon or bully others just to get your way.

Travis I. Sivart

8. Confidence

Confidence is one of the most attractive things a person can possess. I don't mean the swagger and false egotism that makes people look at you. I mean truly understanding what you're worth, and we are all worth more than we know.

Physically, this may be as simple as pulling your shoulders back, and looking people in the eye. A firm handshake and voice helps a lot too. Speaking to the point and not beating around the bush is another way to show your confidence. Don't hem and haw, that makes folks think you don't know what you want.

Travis I. Sivart

9. Forgive & Forget More

Don't hold onto anger, discontentment, and emotional pain. That is the point of forgiving and forgetting. It is not the literal act of blinding yourself to someone who does bad things to you. That would be idiocy. But when you can forgive, it is a release for you. You take away the power that person has over you by removing their control over your anger or fear.

As for forgetting, this is the process of moving on, not removing the event from your memory. Don't let one event or act stop you from taking risks in that area ever again. Like with forgiving though, don't keep making the same mistake again and again, or put yourself into the same situation.

This is all about peace of mind and not carrying emotional baggage that stops you from enjoying new things, not about letting one person repeatedly abuse you. Leave that person or situation in the past, and move on. That is forgiving and forgetting.

Travis I. Sivart

10. Stand Up for Yourself

Standing up for yourself can take many forms. But I feel it can be summed up in one simple phrase; don't let yourself be used by others.

As a child I was smaller than the other kids, and I got picked on for it. Often this would be the bigger kid shoving me or knocking me down. I would stand right back up and look him in the eyes. Of course, I usually said something too, and then he usually knocked me down again. I am not saying this was the smartest course of action for me to take, but I did it anyway. Every single time, someone else stepped in and things settled down.

In life, it is not always that simple or obvious when you're being taken advantage of. Sometimes it is someone at work or home who asks you to do a task that isn't your responsibility. Doing it once to be nice is fine, even a good thing. But if you end up doing it every time, then they are taking advantage of you. To stand up for yourself, you don't have to create a confrontation. Sometimes it's as simple as walking away.

Travis I. Sivart

11. Face Your Fears

Facing your fears can be one of the most difficult things you ever do. It can take the form of sitting in a dark room, asking someone to have coffee with you, or just pushing through your anxiety to do a task that should be a simple, daily event like returning something at a store. Don't jump off a building to get over your fear of heights, but do use a step stool to get something off the top shelf.

The reason it is important to face your fears is not to banish that fear, but to show yourself that you can do it. When you want to, you can overcome anything to get something you want. This is a healthy thing.

Travis I. Sivart

12. Don't Pursue What Runs Away

I am a huge proponent for pursuing your dreams, and often say you can't fail unless you give up. But, some things run away from you. You'll never pet a cat if you chase it. It has to come to you, or at least meet you half way.

This advice most often applies to matters of the heart. If you make your interest known, and that person doesn't meet you half way, then don't pursue them. They will only run faster. And if they appear to be interested, but retreat every time you come closer to them (not necessarily physically), then they are probably playing games with you for their own ego's sake. Or they don't know how to express that they aren't interested and don't want to hurt you. Don't pursue that. Move on and find something that is healthier.

Travis I. Sivart

13. Live in the Moment

This is so important. We all have a past, and it's good to reminisce, and learn from our previous successes and failures. We all have a future, and it's good to plan and hope for what's coming. But you can't live in the past or the future. That's self-destructive.

Living in the moment is a great way to release stress. Most stress comes from regret of the past, or fear of the future. By realizing what's going on right now, right this second, you can enjoy life.

Travis I. Sivart

14. Be Aware of Your Surroundings

The reason this is important advice is two-fold. One, being aware of your surroundings allows you to avoid dangers. That may be tripping over the bump in the sidewalk, or avoiding the shady looking character searching for trouble. Two, it allows you to enjoy what's around you; whether it's birds singing, a pretty cloud, a funny sign, or anything else that may bring a moment of joy.

It's the little things in life that make up the big things.

Travis I. Sivart

15. Learn to Listen

Learning when to stop talking and listen instead is an invaluable skill that will serve you well your whole life. This isn't tuning out while daydreaming so the other person can ramble on about crap you don't care about. This is active listening, which means mentally going through the information as it is given to you.

This can be used in school, at work, or even with a friend. It allows you to glean more information, ask leading questions to dig deeper, and most importantly, help someone by actually listening to what they are saying and their meaning.

So many people never have a conversation. Instead, they catch one tidbit of information, then mentally loop the response they want to give, and aren't listening at all. They are just waiting for their chance to spout more crap. Most folks who talk want to be heard. That's all they want. They want to know you heard what they are saying. Their fears, dreams, silly jokes, crazy ideas, extreme opinions, and whatever else they spout out.

Active listening deepens the bond between two people, and gives so much to the speaker, as well as the listener.

Travis I. Sivart

16. Know What You Want

How can you ever do anything you want, or succeed if you never even know what you want? Perhaps right now, you're muttering that you do know what you want. Well? Go on, tell yourself what you want. Start with today, what do you want out of this day, or what did you want to accomplish? Now what about this month? This year? The next decade? In fifty years?

Yes, get all that info from yourself. Oh wait, let me reassure you – it's ok to not know. Realizing that you don't know is the first step to figuring it out. Also, allow the answers to change as you grow and change. But without a goal, aka knowing what you want, how can you accomplish anything?

This goes from something simple like; I want to make one person smile, or I want to make money today, to huge amazing things like; I want to write a book, or travel to another country. Obviously, some things can be daily goals, others are longer term goals and deserve to be given more time to come to fruition.

In the simplest of reason to know what you want – even if it is just pizza, or Chinese, for dinner – is because people respect and follow someone who knows what they want. Choose to lead, or decide to follow someone else who knows what they want.

Travis I. Sivart

17. Stay Clean, Dress Neatly

When I was sixteen and living on my own with a twenty-seven year old roommate in New York, he said something that stuck with me; always look your best, even if you're covered in paint and wearing work clothes. See, we did painting, tile working, wallpapering, and other such tasks. And I would watch this man, even when a mess from working, step up to another person and have an air of confidence that made the other person notice him.

    I know I already covered confidence, but this is an extension of that. Dress neatly, let's start with that. This means don't look like crap. How do I explain this in one page? Look your best within the circumstances you are in. Tuck in your shirt, stand up straight, wear clean clothes, or whatever you can to show folks that you know what you're doing. Never be the slob. Slovenly behavior or appearance gives the impression that you don't care about yourself; and if you don't care about yourself, why should anyone else? Even in the torn jeans, rebellious phase, you can still be clean and neat. That may sound like it is at odds with one another, but it isn't.

Travis I. Sivart

18. Learn to Speak

This is so important; I cannot express this vague and confusing, what-the-hell-do-you-mean concept enough. So, let's see if I can explain it so you get it.

When I was fourteen years old, a young lady and I were walking down the street. I was complimenting her, and said, "Your voice is like, I don't know, I can't describe it." And she replied, "Yes you can, Travis, you can describe anything." And I realized she was right. So to close the story, I said her voice sounded like a pink, fluffy cloud.

The point is that knowing how to express yourself verbally is invaluable. You don't have to be elegant or poetic, just able to do it. How do you accomplish this? I will give you a few ideas.

Slow down. Collect your thoughts, organize them, and then lay them out in front of the other person in a very clear manner.

Keep it simple. Don't go into the details too much, others will grow bored and begin picking it apart. Let them create the details that work for them. The point is to get your meaning across, not make a long dissertation to make them be in awe of you.

Realize when someone isn't listening. When you feel you must repeat yourself, when they don't follow your whole thought but argue one point you made in the beginning, or a bazillion other things… stop talking. They aren't listening. You made your point, let it rest.

Travis I. Sivart

19. Be Prepared

Got a handkerchief? No? Why not? They're small, compact, and have a bunch of uses. They can be used to clean a windshield, mop up a spill, bind a wound, blow your nose when you can't find a tissue or napkin, but the most common use is to give it (not lend, but give) to a woman who is crying.

Being prepared is a wide and varied piece of advice, which I would clarify with, you cannot be prepared for every eventuality. But you can carry a few things that allow you to be ready for many different things, and this goes for men or women, (even the hanky thing). In the physical side of things; carry a pocketknife, loose change, small screwdriver, lighter, or anything else you think you may have some use for more than four times a year. Ok, don't go crazy, but it's easy enough to have a pen and paper ready as opposed to other things. Have a jack in your car, a cell phone allows you to have a calculator, compass, etc. Multi-tools are cheap and portable.

You can never be prepared for everything, but you can have a general readiness.

Travis I. Sivart

20. Know Three Clean Jokes

This is something I used to phrase as, know three jokes you could tell to your grandmother. But today's grandmothers aren't the same saintly, silver-haired, innocent, little old ladies that we used to think of in my childhood. In this current day and age, they may also be silver-haired, tattooed, raise-a-shot-and-drink-to-your-health, tell-you-to-go-screw-yourself, woman that is the modern strong lady.

So, I advise that you know three clean jokes that you can tell among strangers that may be kindergarteners, church-going believers, or whatever.

Why should you do this? Because humor is universal, and creating a bond with laughter is invaluable. Now, go learn about the horse that walked into the bar, and the bartender said, "Why the long face?"

Travis I. Sivart

21. Understand Your Goals, Large & Small

Oh, where do I start on this? Ok, so I mentioned this in a couple of other places. Let me break it down; goals are not one huge thing, they are many small things. Quick example; you want to skydive and parachute. This is more than one step, such as; save money, research a place, set up an appointment, do the pre-jump stuff, do the jump, post to social media, etc.

What I just showed you is a large goal, broken up into many smaller goals. A large goal can become overwhelming and intimidating. But if you break it into manageable bites, it's easier to digest and accomplish.

My point is don't let a large goal become too much for you. Break it into smaller goals, which make you feel like you have succeeded in each step, and encourages you to complete the larger achievement.

Travis I. Sivart

22. Clean as You Go

Really, follow this as a rule in everything you do. I'll compare it to your home, apartment, and even your car. Don't let things pile up, they become a mess. If you put things in the trash, and take it out before it's full, then you never have trash everywhere. If you organize things – dirty clothes, mail, dirty dishes, or whatever – and take care of them on a regular basis (ok, I mean daily) then they never can overwhelm you.

Spending five minutes to clean your dishes is easier than thirty minutes with an overflowing sink. Taking in one fast food bag full of trash from the day's travel is easier than digging through a pile of trash in your car floorboard that comes to your knees, etc.

This goes for all kinds of things, not just your home and car. This rule applies to emotional and mental issues too. Don't let them build up to overwhelming proportions. But only you can take care of it before it becomes a tidal wave and makes you want to run for a hiding place.

Travis I. Sivart

23. Avoid Extremes & Excess

In all things, avoid extremes and excess. I've had too many friends ruin their lives to drugs, food, video games, or obsessive behavior over their love interest because of extremes and excess.

Don't do it.

Realize a healthy life is a balance. There's not all or nothing, black or white, right or wrong. Everything is made up of layers and spectrums and not just two things.

I can't make this simpler than I have. If you don't get it in what you just read, then enjoy the recovery from your chosen addiction.

Travis I. Sivart

24. Succeed & Fail with Grace

I guarantee you will succeed in some things, and fail in others. This may be as simplistic as a game or discussion, or as complex as a career or a love relationship. Learn to succeed and fail without creating drama around what you've done.

Some folks feel the need to draw attention to their selves and let folks know how urgent, important, and paramount their peak or valley in life has been. Don't be that person. Your friends will celebrate or commiserate these events, as appropriate, but if you think the world needs to know or care, you have just crossed a line that will make you more of a tabloid headline than an emotionally excited or interesting individual.

Personal success or failure is meant to be supported by your inner circle, not the whole world. The sooner you learn that, the better your support structure will be. By the way, ringing that bell too often is akin to the boy that cried wolf. Don't do it just because you have the urge to get a little attention, no matter the cost.

Travis I. Sivart

25. Use Manners & Common Courtesy

Please, thank you, yes sir, no ma'am, holding the door for a stranger, etc. goes further than you may ever know. For the most part this is a seamless and invisible habit, a thankless task. But in the long run, those most often around you will form an opinion about your grace and personal character.

More importantly is the effect is has on you as an individual, and your own self-worth. Don't hesitate to be courteous for your own sake. If that doesn't make sense, then let me put it this way; this is a silent investment in your own character and self-worth. Be the person who finds small pleasure in helping others in inconsequential ways. Because, it actually makes a huge difference in your unconscious view of yourself.

Travis I. Sivart

26. Breathe, Hydrate, & Sleep

Three of the most basic things in any animal - and we are still animals no matter what we may think – is to drink plenty, sleep enough, and breathe deeply.

Sleep is one of the most important things to thinking clearly and being ready to face any challenge the day may present.

Drinking enough WATER – not soda, coffee, or whatever – makes you physically able to function.

Breathing; oh, where do I start with this? Getting the proper amount of oxygen to your body effects everything you do. Breathe deeply when stressed or anxious, making yourself take multiple – at least ten – deep breaths allows you to think clearly and respond better.

This is science, folks. Look it up. Sleep enough, drink enough, and breathe right.

Travis I. Sivart

27. Time Management

Being successful in anything - personal, professional, or anything else – is time management. Whether you're waiting tables, setting up a home, or writing a book, it's a matter of realizing that there are only so many hours in the day, and so many minutes in each hour.

Setting your schedule so you're the most productive you can be is the key to being who you want to be. There is nothing wrong with wasting time enjoying pleasure activities, as long as it is balanced with doing the things that move you forward in life.

Make lists or schedules, and sticking to them is the key to getting what you want. No one else will do this for you.

Travis I. Sivart

Enjoying what you're reading?
Want a free eBook?

Go to
http://www.TravisISivart.com/FreeBook

Travis I. Sivart

About the Author

Travis I. Sivart lives in a state of constant flux between Richmond, VA and Washington, DC with his son and cats. He is not just an author but also father, public speaker, cook, pipe smoker, cat & squirrel lover, internet radio host, and so much more.

Travis I. Sivart is a Jack-Of-All-Trades. He has worked in mundane jobs such as restaurants, retail, construction, DMV, Notary, tech help, and more as well as exotic trades such as; singing pirate, exorcist and paranormal researcher, Duke, cigar and pipe connoisseur, master of dungeons, a knight, therapist, minister, King, and has degrees in religion and metaphysics.

Travis I. Sivart writes steampunk, social DIY, science fiction, fantasy, young adult, speculative fiction, horror, and more.

You can find Travis at www.TravisISivart.com.

Travis I. Sivart

If you enjoyed this book…

Please let others know by reviewing it on Amazon or Goodreads, and let others know your thoughts!

Other books by Travis I. Sivart:

27 Thoughts on Enjoying Life

Travis I. Sivart draws on his lifetime of helping other to offer his personal guidelines for enjoying life. This book offers twenty-seven thoughts on helping create happiness in your personal life, success in your professional life, and even manage depression on a daily basis by suggesting ways to improve and maintain your mental, physical, and emotional well-being.

Steampunk For Simpletons: A Fun Primer For Folks Who Aren't Sure What Steampunk Is All About

A primer followed by a guided tour through the world of steampunk, from the basics such as where to go and what to do, to the aesthetic of the arts within steampunk.

Journal of a Stranger

The thoughts, ideas, philosophies, and inspirations of a time traveling adventurer. Delving into the psychology of man, life's eternal questions, burning passions, and the quirky pseudo-science of his mind, and more.

27 Thoughts about Steampunk

Travis I. Sivart draws on his passion of steampunk as an aesthetic and a hobby to offer his personal insights for helping others to begin delving into this fascinating culture and genre. This book offers twenty-seven thoughts on the basic questions and concepts that often crop up when someone is beginning to explore this incredible movement.

Travis I. Sivart

27 Thoughts on Having No Regrets in Life

Travis I. Sivart